MINING THE MEANING OF THE BIBLE

Beyond the Literal Word

SALLIE LATKOVICH, CSJ

Liguori
LIGUORI, MIS

Imprimi Potest: Harry Grile, CSsR
Provincial, Denver Province, The Redemptorists

Published by Liguori Publications, Liguori, Missouri 63057
To order, call 800-325-9521 or visit www.liguori.org

Copyright © 2011 Sallie Latkovich, CSJ

Library of Congress Cataloging-in-Publication Data
Latkovich, Sallie.
    Mining the meaning of the Bible : beyond the literal word / Sallie Latkovich.
        p. cm.
    ISBN 978-0-7648-1982-7
    1. Bible—Introductions. 2. Bible—Liturgical use. 3. Catholic Church—Liturgy. I. Title.
    BS475.3.L37 2011
    220.6′1--dc22

                                        2010040542

Printed in the United States of America
15 14 13 12 11 10   5 4 3 2 1
First edition

Contents

FOREWORD

A few years ago, my niece, Nancy, was about to celebrate her birthday. I wanted to get her a gift, maybe a book. Her dad asked me, "Do you know about any books that would help Nancy understand the Bible? She is full of questions about it."

I knew I could find something. I had a lot of catalogs at home with books like that...or at least I thought I did. There were lots of Bibles for kids, but no books that would help Nancy understand the Bible. So, I decided to write a book for Nancy—and for you—so we could go mining for the treasures in the Bible. I gave it to her at her birthday party. She read it aloud. Then all the people who heard her said they wanted a copy.

After that, I shared my book with a lot of other people I knew. I began to use the book in classes, presentations, and workshops for adults: catechists, pastoral ministers, adult education groups in parishes, and people enrolled in Rite of Christian Initiation for Adults (RCIA) classes.

In my presentations, I noted that the Bible is a whole library of books. The word "bible" comes from the Greek word *biblos*. It simply means "books." The word "Scripture," which means "sacred writings," is often used to describe it as well.

When we are gathered with people of the Christian faith, people who believe in God, or people who have come together to worship, we hear readings from the Bible. It is in this gathering when passages from these books are read aloud that we believe that the Bible is the word of God. The first part of the Mass is the Liturgy of the Word. The reader (whom we call the lector) proclaims the passages from the Bible, and they are told in such a way that people want to listen; they want to hear the word of God. That means we understand these books to be very important, and they are the way that God speaks to us.

> THE OLD FAMILIAR
> ADAGE SAYS:
> "GIVE A PERSON A
> FISH, AND HE EATS
> FOR A DAY.
> TEACH A PERSON TO
> FISH, AND HE EATS
> FOR A LIFETIME."

May this simple book be a beginning for many who will be nourished in their lifetimes by the word of God.

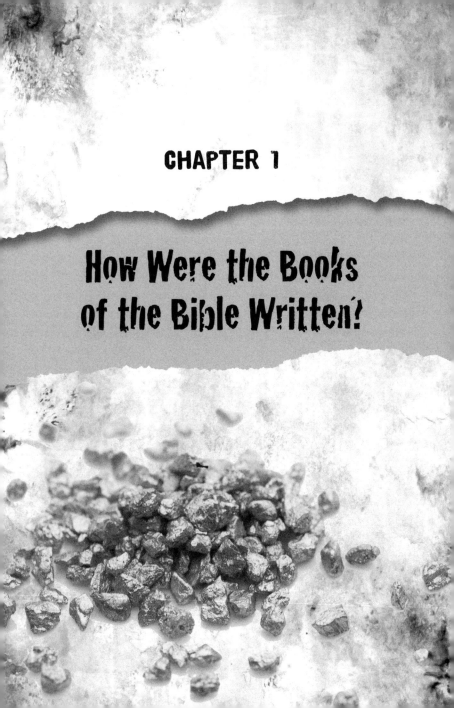

CHAPTER 1

How Were the Books of the Bible Written?

At first, the books of the Bible weren't books at all. Remember, ancient people didn't have radios, TVs, or newspapers; and certainly no Internet, YouTube, Facebook, cell phones, or texting.

So the only way people knew what was going on was by passing the word to each other, and by telling the stories over and over. This is called the oral tradition. That's how the stories were passed down. So the stories of the Bible were stories of faith, rooted in history and, importantly, inspired by God.

As everyone talked, especially about the stories they didn't understand, they tried to figure out what the stories meant. What were the people supposed to learn from them? All stories teach us something, right? In the Bible, the details of the historical events in a story weren't as important as what God was saying and doing.

In fact, when the ancient people heard the stories, they would ask: "What is God saying to us?" The stories stirred up faith in their hearts. They didn't just know more about God; they knew God better.

So as time went on, friends and families talked about the meanings of the stories. They prayed together to understand the stories better, and of course, they continued to tell the stories. Some stories were told in order to teach us something or explain some aspect of the world and how God relates to us, but the stories not only explained who they were, but also taught about God and why and how God acted on their behalf.

Finally, after a very long time, people—upon being inspired by God—decided to write the stories down. They were afraid the stories would be forgotten, and they knew that the stories would be preserved and saved if they were written. Today, we know those people of faith were right, because we have those same stories in written form.

It is crucial to remember that God inspired the authors to write the books that we believe to be God's word. And, just like those people thousands of years ago, when we read or hear Bible stories, we want to know what they mean. Trying to understand the stories is a process. It is just like a miner panning for gold. That process takes effort, hard work, and persistence. You have to sift through many parts to find the true gold, to dig to deeper levels, each with its own meaning. These stories have God's inspirational message for us.

Let's review how the Bible came to be written:

- People noticed what was happening in their lives and in their world.
- With inspiration from God, the people then reflected on these events, looking for the meaning of God's actions.
- The meanings became the most important parts of the stories as they were passed down within families and from one generation to the next.
- These God-inspired stories and their meanings were written so that people would not forget them.

God's messages for us are in the Bible, but we must work to mine their meaning. We must look beyond the literal words and go to deeper and deeper levels to understand the meaning.

Peoples of the Old Testament

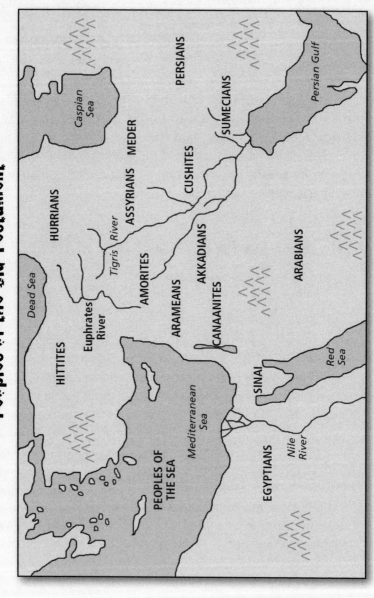

Caspian Sea

Dead Sea

HURRIANS

HITTITES

Tigris River

Euphrates River

ASSYRIANS

MEDER

PERSIANS

AMORITES

ARAMEANS

AKKADIANS

CUSHITES

SUMECIANS

Persian Gulf

CANAANITES

Mediterranean Sea

PEOPLES OF THE SEA

SINAI

ARABIANS

Red Sea

Nile River

EGYPTIANS

Israel's Neighboring Cities

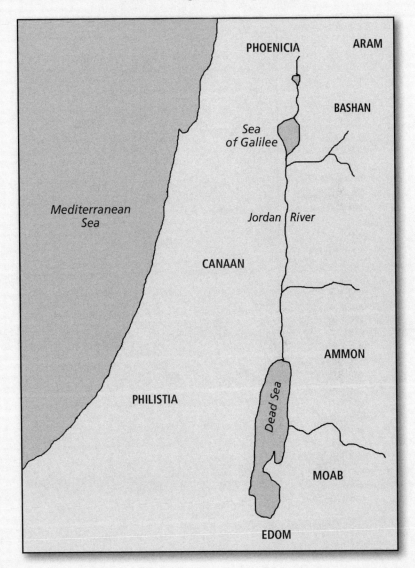

Important Places in the Life of Jesus

1. Nazareth
   Luke 1–2

2. Bethlehem
   Luke 2:11

3. Jordan
   Matthew 3:13

4. Sea of Galilee
   Mark 1:16–19

5. Cana
   John 2:1–11

6. Sea of Galilee
   Matthew 14:22–23

7. Sychar
   John 4:5

8. Capernaum
   John 6:17

9. Nain
   Luke 7:11–17

10. Bethsaida
    Luke 9:10–17

11. Caesarea-Phillipi
    Mark 8:27

12. Mount Tabor
    Mark 9:2

13. Jericho
    *Mark 10:46–52;
    and Luke 19:1–10*

14. Bethany
    John 11:1–44

15. Jerusalem
    John 19 and Matthew 28

16. Emmaus
    Luke 24:13–35

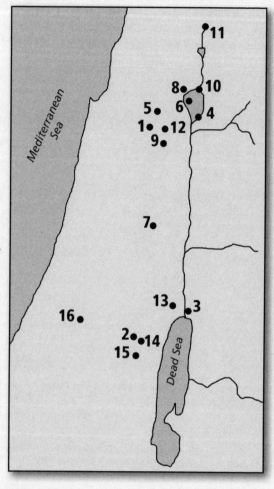

Christianity in the First Century

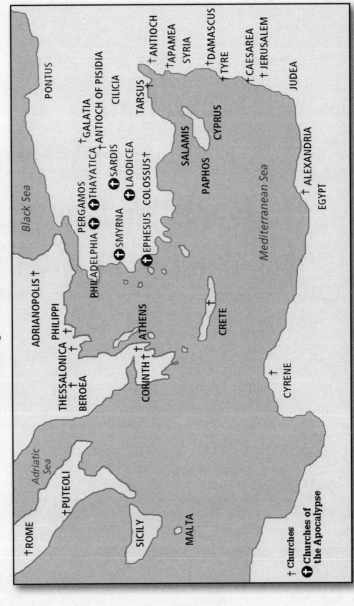

† Churches
ⓣ Churches of the Apocalypse

Black Sea

Mediterranean Sea

Adriatic Sea

PONTUS

† ANTIOCH
† APAMEA
SYRIA
† DAMASCUS
† TYRE
† CAESAREA
† JERUSALEM
JUDEA

TARSUS †
CILICIA
† ANTIOCH OF PISDIA
† GALATIA
PERGAMOS ⓣ ⓣ THAYATICA
ⓣ SARDIS
SMYRNA ⓣ
PHILADELPHIA ⓣ ⓣ LAODICEA
ⓣ EPHESUS COLOSSUS †

SALAMIS
CYPRUS
PAPHOS
† ALEXANDRIA
EGYPT

ADRIANOPLIS †
PHILIPPI †
THESSALONICA †
BEROEA †
ATHENS †
CORINTH †
CRETE †
CYRENE †

† ROME
† PUTEOLI
SICILY
MALTA

13

CHAPTER 2

Words We Use
and What They Mean

The Bible is divided into two main sections—the Old Testament and the New Testament. Everything in the Old Testament took place before the birth of Christ. The New Testament focuses on the life of Christ and the early Christian Church.

The first part of the Bible contains stories of the people of ancient Israel, the Hebrews. Some of the Old Testament books were written hundreds of years after the events took place. People told the stories over and over, and later on decided to write them down. Some of the "events" described in the Old Testament did not really happen. They are theological stories rooted in history, but they have a meaning to tell. It is the meaning that is true. That is why we search for the meaning.

The New Testament is occasionally referred to as the Christian Bible because it is still very old. The first Gospels about Jesus' life were written almost forty years after his death and resurrection, which took place about two thousand years ago.

GOSPEL

The word "gospel" means "good news." That is why we sing "Alleluia" before we hear the Gospel at Mass. Singing the "Alleluia" is a chance to praise God because we are about to hear the Good News. The four Gospels are all stories of Jesus, his life, his teaching, his miracles, and his death and resurrection. So, stories of Jesus are always Good News!

Sometimes, the Gospel doesn't sound like Good News. It is not always easy to live the way Jesus wants us to. But the Gospel is always Good News for everyone, including the poor or those who are rejected or turned away by society. Jesus never ignored them—or anyone else—and his Good News of eternal salvation won't, either.

TRANSLATION AND INTERPRETATION

Do you have friends who speak a language different from yours? When they speak that other language, someone has to translate the language for you. Translators help us understand the words of another language and culture while at the same time trying to retain the meaning of the original texts; they help make the world one.

Interpreters do much the same thing. Not only do they make sure that one language is translated correctly, they make sure the real meaning comes across in the translation.

Any Bible written in English is always a translation from another language. The books of the Bible have been translated from the languages of the ancient Near East and Hebrew and from Greek and Aramaic.

> **A GOOD TRANSLATION HELPS US TO UNDERSTAND THE REAL MEANING, BUT A BAD TRANSLATION CAN LEAD TO MISUNDERSTANDINGS.**

Some of the English Bibles we have were first translated from those ancient languages into Latin, French, or German. Then someone translated them again, into English. That can make the stories even more difficult to understand. Today most of our English Bibles were translated directly from the original languages of the Bible.

Translating from one language to another is hard to do. A good translation helps us to understand the real meaning, but a bad translation can lead to misunderstandings. That's why an interpretation that communicates the real meaning is so important.

Here is an example from the Bible. In Chapter 8 of Mark's Gospel, verse 31, Jesus is telling his disciples about his death and resurrection. For the disciples, this must have been really hard news to get. It was hard for them, and it is hard for us to think of our Messiah as having to suffer and die. In most translations of this story, Peter takes Jesus aside to "rebuke" him. This sounds like when your parents take you aside to correct you for saying something wrong. A translator chose the word "rebuke," but a similar word may have made more sense. In a different translation—or interpretation—of the same story, it says Peter took Jesus aside to "silence" him.

From what you know about the friendship between Jesus and Peter, which choice sounds right to you? Wouldn't it have been natural for Peter to try to get Jesus to stop speaking about his death? Of course. Translations can be tricky; even one word can change a story's meaning. But thanks to Roman Catholic interpretations, the Bible maintains its essential meanings.

CATECHISM REFERENCES ON SACRED SCRIPTURE

*Through all the words of Sacred Scripture, God speaks only one single Word, his one Utterance in whom he expresses himself completely:64

> You recall that one and the same Word of God extends throughout Scripture, that it is one and the same Utterance that resounds in the mouths of all the sacred writers, since he who was in the beginning God with God has no need of separate syllables; for he is not subject to time. 65

For this reason, the Church has always venerated the Scriptures as she venerates the Lord's Body. She never ceases to present to the faithful the bread of life, taken from the one table of God's Word and Christ's Body. 66 (CCC, 102–103)

*In Sacred Scripture, the Church constantly finds her nourishment and her strength, for she welcomes it not as a human word, "but as what it really is, the word of God".67 "In the sacred books, the Father who is in heaven comes lovingly to meet his children, and talks with them." 68 (CCC, 104)

64 Cf. Heb 1:1-3
65 St. Augustine, En. in Ps. 103, 4, 1: PL 37, 1378; cf. Ps 104; Jn 1:1
66 Cf. DV 21.
67 Th 2:13; cf. DV 24.
68 DV 21.

*God inspired the human authors of the sacred books. "To compose the sacred books, God chose certain men who, all the while he employed them in this task, made full use of their own faculties and powers so that, though he acted in them and by them, it was as true authors that they consigned to writing whatever he wanted written, and no more." 71 (CCC 106)

*In Sacred Scripture, God speaks to man in a human way. To interpret Scripture correctly, the reader must be attentive to what the human authors truly wanted to affirm, and to what God wanted to reveal to us by their words. 75 (CCC 109)

*"And such is the force and power of the Word of God that it can serve the Church as her support and vigour, and the children of the Church as strength for their faith, food for the soul, and a pure and lasting fount of spiritual life."109 Hence "access to Sacred Scripture ought to be open wide to the Christian faithful." 110 (CCC 131)

71 DV 11.
75 Cf. DV 12 # 1.
109 DV 21.
110 DV 22.
ellos" (DV 21). (CIC 104)

CHAPTER 3

Meanings for People of Different Times and Cultures

The books of the Bible were written in times, places, and cultures that were very different from our own, so we may not understand everything about how people lived back then, even if we want to. We certainly can learn about those differences though, and we should if we want to mine the meaning. One advantage we have in learning the differences is that, no matter what time period we examine, God is always the same. He is constant.

But to learn about other people who lived in other times of history takes some study. This knowledge and understanding will take some time.

Symbolism of Time and Numbers

One difference has to do with time. We think of time very differently now than people did in the ancient world. We have years, months, days, hours, and minutes. We wear watches and have clocks in our homes and offices. We are so specific about time that we even measure things down to the second. In the Bible, though, time often had symbolic importance. Here are some examples:

40 In the Book of Genesis, there is a well-known story about Noah and the ark. God calls Noah to build an ark for himself, his family, and two kinds of every animal. Then it rains for forty days and nights. At the end of

the rains, the earth is renewed and recreated; evil has been conquered and goodness remains. Thus, there was a great change; we sometimes call this "transformation."

The Book of Exodus says that it took forty years for the Jews to wander through the desert until they reached the Promised Land. We hear that and we think they spent exactly forty years in the desert. But really it just meant that several generations had passed. "Forty years" meant that the Jews lived in the desert so long that they had children and even grandchildren before they found their way out.

Most importantly, the number forty became a symbolic number of changes. When we find the number forty in a Bible story, we know that the people in that story have been changed, just like the Israelites who reached the Promised Land and started a new life. They were changed or transformed from slaves in Egypt to free people in the Promised Land.

Think about Jesus, who spent forty days in the desert, praying. He was changed, too. He hadn't been recognized in public healing and teaching before he went to the desert. But after his forty days there, Jesus began his ministry with people. Forty days brought a new beginning for him. We cherish this ancient meaning of forty.

The number seven is also symbolic. First, there were seven days of God's creating in the Book of Genesis. The people of ancient Israel came to believe that seven was a "perfect" number. They saw it as God's number. Because of this belief, they assigned the number seven to whatever they wanted to be "perfect" in their creation. For example, they made seven days in a week. Seven meant perfection.

12 The number twelve means something, too; it means completeness. There were twelve tribes of Israel, so the ancient Israelites saw the number twelve as the special number of God's Chosen People. We also know Jesus chose twelve disciples in the Gospel. And after the feeding of the multitudes, they gathered twelve baskets of leftovers. Like the number seven, the Bible uses the number twelve as a symbol. Twelve shows that God is playing a part in our lives here on earth.

THE 3RD DAY Any event that happens "on the third day" is an event of resurrection, an event of God's raising someone up to new life.

Did you know that the wedding feast at Cana in John's Gospel was a "third day" event? The story begins like this: "On the third day there was a wedding at Cana in Galilee..." We know the story well: they ran out of wine, and Mary calls on Jesus to do something. Jesus has the servants fill the large jars with water, and when it is tasted, the water has become wine. Jesus was "raised up" as he changed the water into wine. We might say that he saved the day. In John's Gospel, this was the first of the signs; and people also changed as they came to believe.

In another part of the Gospels, one of Jesus' dear friends dies. His name was Lazarus. Upon Lazarus' death, Jesus waited for the third day to go to him, and when he got there, Jesus called him forth from his grave. He truly raised Lazarus from the dead on the third day, and while it was a foreshadowing of Jesus' resurrection, this was another important event that caused people to believe in Jesus.

Finally, as we know so well, Jesus himself was raised up to new life on the third day after his death on the cross.

Symbolism of Numbers in the Bible

1 The one and only God, divinity and greatness. We have one God. "Hear, O Israel! The LORD is our God, the LORD alone!" (Deuteronomy 6:4).

2 Deceitfulness, disagreement, division, opposition, and complementary. It is the basis of community. God created the brighter light to govern the day and the lesser light to govern the night (Genesis 1:16), "No one can serve two masters. He will either hate one and love the other, or be devoted to one and despise the other" (Matthew 6:24).

3 "And be ready for the third day; for on the third day the LORD will come down on Mount Sinai before the eyes of all the people" (Exodus 19:11). Divine perfection, reconciliation of duality, analogy to the Trinity. "So will the Son of Man be in the heart of the earth three days and three nights" (Matthew 12:40).

4 Human reality and cosmic unity. For example, if one speaks of the four rivers of paradise (Genesis 2:10–14), it refers to the entire cosmos or world.

7 Seven is the number of perfection, and it is used to express wholeness or completeness. "I say to you, not seven times but seventy-seven times" (Matthew 18:22).

10 This is another expression of completeness. It is mentioned where the message includes everything that is possible in those circumstances. For example: the Ten Commandments (Exodus 20:1–17), and Job complaining that he had been insulted ten times (Job 19:3). Praise to God is made on a ten-stringed harp (Psalm 92:4). Jesus cures ten lepers (Luke 17:17). Jesus teaches a parable about ten virgins (Matthew 25:1).

---

12 This is a social number. This is why there are twelve tribes of Israel, twelve apostles, and twelve baskets of leftovers after the multiplying of the loaves (John 6:13). Twelve deals with the selection of people in social organizations.

---

40 The number forty indicates a profound and radical change in life. There were forty days of rain that resulted in the Great Flood (Genesis 7:4,12,17). The Israelites spent forty years wandering in the desert and eating manna (Exodus 16:35). Moses spent forty days on Mount Sinai when he went to receive the tablets of the Law (Exodus 24:18 and 34:28). Solomon's reign lasted for forty years (2 Chronicles 9:30). Jesus spent forty days in the desert (Matthew 4:2, Mark 1:13, Luke 4:2). The risen Jesus appeared for forty days (Acts 4:22).

OUR CONTINUED USE OF
THE TRADITIONAL SYMBOLS

We can see that a lot of the numbers in the Bible have a deeper meaning. We remember and express those meanings in the traditions of our Church. For example, in our Catholic tradition, we have seven sacraments. We have also picked up the theme of forty days in our Church's calendar. As the people of God, we have a special season each year when we pray to be changed: to be more holy, more like the people God created us to be, more like Jesus. This is Lent, and it lasts for forty days each year. At the end of the forty days, we have a great new beginning in the resurrection of Jesus that we celebrate each Easter. We are changed.

When we read or hear the Bible, then, it is very important to seek the meaning or the message that is from God. Our Church traditions often help us to understand or interpret the message. In this way, we learn more about God and more about ourselves.

Symbolism of Places

Because the first meeting of God with Moses took place on Mount Sinai, any important "meeting" with God happens on a mountain in the Bible. Some places are called "mountains" when there is no geographic mountain there; it tells us that the event is an important meeting with God.

For example, a famous section of Matthew's Gospel is called "The Sermon on the Mount." It begins with the Beatitudes and says, "When Jesus saw the crowds, he went up the mountain." If you visit the northern end of the Sea of Galilee today, you would say a hill is there, but certainly no mountain. The meaning is that the Beatitudes and the whole sermon come from God.

So if you are in your family's home, in church, or in your

classroom and feel that you have met God in your prayer, you might say that you, too, were on the mountain—even though a real mountain may not be there.

In a similar way, water is very important in the Gospels. Now, there are real bodies of water in Israel/Palestine: the Sea of Galilee, the Jordan River, and the Dead Sea. But water often means baptism. In the fourth Gospel (John), there is a story of a Samaritan woman at a well. She has come to draw water, and while there really is a "Jacob's well" from which you can still draw water, the important meaning of the story is a different type of water. Jesus speaks of life-giving water, which is the water of baptism.

In another Gospel story, the disciples are out on their boat, fishing. Peter recognizes that Jesus is on the shore. The Gospel might be a little puzzling when it says that Peter "put on" his shirt and dove into the sea. For sure, we are reminded of the white garment we are given at baptism, when we, too, are immersed in water.

So we must be attentive to the symbolism of time, numbers, and places as we "mine the meaning" of the Bible. These are all important clues to help us to understand why we still tell these stories of ancient people who lived in faraway places. Not only do we understand the stories, but we also take the stories to heart and allow them to shape and form us.

SYMBOLIC PLACES IN THE BIBLE

PLACE	SYMBOLISM
Road/Way	A place to find or meet God.
Field/Ground/Earth	Refers to the world in general, the place where human history develops.
City	Represents society in general, and the communities built by people.
Desert	A place of passage in light of a transformation, but the desert is never permanent.
Mountain	A place to step back from the world to seek or encounter God.
River	In the Old Testament, a sign of division between the gifts of God and the tricks of the Evil One. In the New Testament, a place of purification.
Valley	The opposite of the mountain, a valley is a place of darkness and distance from God.

CHAPTER 4

Styles of Writing

When people read newspapers, or when we visit our favorite websites on the Internet, we are almost unaware of how we read stories differently. We read about a robbery differently than we read about the latest games and gadgets, and we read the sports differently than we read about our favorite musicians and actors. Each story has its own style.

In the same way, when we go to the library or to a bookstore, the books are organized into sections that help us find what we are looking for. There are different styles of writing in the different books of the Bible as well. If we know the different styles, we'll know how to read and to listen to them. Knowing the styles may even help us find what we are looking for in the Bible.

The simplest writing style is narrative. A story is told, and we read or hear it, paying attention to its meaning. The meaning is usually about God and often about us. Another style in the Bible is storytelling. These important stories may not be completely and historically accurate, but their meaning is real and their message is true. Each story is trying to communicate a message.

Poetry is also used in the Bible, and poetry has imagery. A poem paints pictures in your mind to tell you a story in a different way, and we have to figure out what the images and metaphors mean. It helps if we pay attention to what we feel as we read the poems. In the Bible, the psalms are poetry. When we sing: "And he will raise you up on eagle's wings...," we know that eagles are not going to swoop down to lift us up, but the very image causes us to feel lifted up by God.

Another type of writing that is used in the Gospels is parable. Parables are more than nice stories that Jesus told and used in his teaching. Every parable has a "gotcha." This part of the story makes us stop and notice the way we think, what we believe, and how we live. Parables usually leave us with a challenge as we try to follow Jesus and live as he did.

For example, Jesus once told a parable about workers who were hired to work in a vineyard, the place where wine grapes are grown. The owner hired some of the workers in the morning, some at noon, some in the late afternoon. So some of the workers were hard at it all day. Others worked a half-day, and some only a few hours. It came time for the workers to be paid and Jesus said that all of the workers received the same amount of money. We'd probably say, "That's not fair."

Jesus was trying to teach us about the generosity of God, and that God rewards each of us in a different way than how we are rewarded here on earth for our work.

God is so loving and generous. God invites everyone to be part of the team; to work in God's kingdom. Are we so generous? That's the "gotcha." We are challenged to think and to act like God does.

Styles of Writing in the Old Testament

Narrative: Telling of stories

Historical writings: Reporting meaningful history

Discourse: A speech

Prophecies: Statements of criticism; signs of things to come

Canticles: Hymns, songs

Wisdom literature: Words, proverbs to live by

Styles of Writing in the New Testament

Narrative: Telling of stories

Parables, comparisons, metaphors: Ways to convey a message

Letters: Documents written to communities

Apocalyptic: Allegorical and symbolic visions

CHAPTER 5

The Bible Is
a Library

We usually don't read the whole Bible from beginning to end. Remember how the Greek word *biblos* means books? The Bible is really a collection of books, a library. In a library, we walk around and pick out books from different places. In the same way that we choose books at the library or bookstore, we choose books of the Bible.

The Bible at Mass

To help us use the whole "library" of the Bible, the Church chooses readings for us to hear when we gather together for Mass and celebrate the Liturgy of the Word. The book that contains those readings from the Bible is known as a Lectionary, or simply a "book of readings." The readings correspond to the liturgical season, or the time of the Church year.

On Sundays, there are always three readings and a psalm. First, we hear a reading from the Old Testament, and then we hear or sing a psalm. The second reading that we hear is from one of the "letters" of the Christian Scriptures. Finally, after our "Alleluia," we hear a story from the Gospels, the stories of Jesus' life. During Mass most of the days of the week, we hear only two readings and a psalm, and over the course of the three-year Lectionary cycle we hear much of the Bible.

THE OLD TESTAMENT

In the Old Testament, the first five books are called the Pentateuch—a word that simply means "five." Those five books contain the stories of creation, God's covenant with Abraham and Sarah in Genesis, the call of Moses, the story of the exodus in Exodus, and the laws of God's people in Numbers, Leviticus, and Deuteronomy. These five books make up the Jewish Torah and are considered by Jews to be the most holy of all the books and oral traditions. They are sometimes referred to as the Law.

The Historical Books that come next contain the history of the people of Israel and the stories of the monarchy or the time of the kings. Among these books are Joshua and Judges, The First and Second Books of Samuel, and the First and Second Books of Kings.

Another group of books is the Wisdom Literature. These books encourage the Israelite people to live wisely in their covenant with God and each other. The Wisdom books are handbooks for life as God's people. Among the Wisdom books are Job, Proverbs, Ecclesiastes, Song of Songs, Wisdom, and Sirach.

When Solomon became king of Israel, God invited him to ask for whatever he wanted. Solomon asked for the gift of wisdom, an understanding heart. Ever since that time, it has been thought that wisdom was God's special gift, and given to kings. (In Matthew's Gospel, we find the story of the Magi: the wonderful story of the men following the star to find the newborn king. We sing: "We three kings of orient are..." Now, Matthew's Gospel doesn't say anything

IN THE MASS, THE BOOK THAT CONTAINS THE READINGS FROM THE BIBLE IS KNOWN AS A LECTIONARY.

about them being kings. The early Christians thought they were very wise and thus called them kings.)

The Book of Psalms is a collection of 150 prayers. Some of the most well- known parts of the Bible are here, like Psalm 23: "The Lord is my shepherd." Many psalms are also popular songs in church, like *Eagle's Wings*, which is Psalm 91 set to music.

Finally, there is a collection of books that we call the Prophets. The prophets were men and women who called the nation of Israel to remain faithful to their covenant with God. Prophets called for justice, which means living in "right relationship" with God and with others, and all of God's creation. There is a

The Creation Accounts

An especially important and well-known part of the Old Testament is the first book, Genesis. It begins with two stories of the creation of the world and people. We don't ask which of the two stories is "right." Nor do we ask, "What really happened?" We do ask, and always ask: "What do they mean?"

In the first story, God creates everything in seven days. There's a treasure of ideas to find in this story. Let's look closely and go mining for the meaning. We find:

God is the Creator of life. God's word is powerful. After all, what God says, happens.

God brings order out of chaos. Night after day, for seven days, God puts everything in order.

God views creation as good, and humans as good.

God makes humans in God's "image," in the image of a creator. In other words, God creates us so that we can create life, too.

The seventh day is given to rest, to Sabbath. The seventh day is a time to remember God and to savor and enjoy the goodness of all of creation.

long list of prophetic books in the Bible. These include: Isaiah, Jeremiah, Lamentations, Baruch, Ezekiel, Daniel, Hosea, Joel, Amos, Obadiah, Jonah, Micah, Nahum, Habakkuk, Zephaniah, Haggai, Zechariah and Malachi.

Another song we hear often has words that come from the prophet Isaiah: it is *Be Not Afraid*. When we sing this song, we are reminded that God's words to Israel are still important to us today.

The second creation story is the famous story of Adam and Eve, the serpent-tempter, and the apple. Don't bother asking, "What really happened?" Instead ask: "What does it mean?" If we look, we can dig out God's message to us.

The story of Adam, Eve, and the serpent reminds us that we all run into temptation, times when we want things that are actually not good for us. It also shows that we all have free will, so we are responsible for our actions, even though it might seem easier to blame someone or something else.

What else does the story mean? Well, the temptation in the story isn't simply about eating an apple. And if we actually take a look at the story we find that there is no mention of an apple, just fruit from the tree of knowledge. Sometimes when we read the stories for ourselves we find out all kinds of interesting things, like the fact that there are two separate creation stories and two different counts on the number of animals on the Ark. The temptation is really that Adam and Eve wanted to be God, to do things their way, not God's way.

This is the most basic human temptation. We even call it "original sin." We crave power, and because of our free will, we're able to make wrong choices. We can betray our relationship with God, our Creator, when we act on the belief that we are God ourselves.

THE NEW TESTAMENT

In the New Testament, most people know the four Gospels—the Good News—best. There are four stories of Jesus, told by Matthew, Mark, Luke, and John. Though they are all about Jesus, they show four different portraits of Jesus, because Matthew, Mark, Luke, and John wrote in different places and times for a variety of communities and people.

The Gospels of Matthew, Mark, and Luke are called the "synoptic Gospels." Synoptic means "same eye." These three Gospels seem to have the same eye, as they tell many of the same stories of Jesus. They are different because of the first hearers, and the meanings that were important to each group.

In the Catholic Church, we have three cycles of readings for our Sunday Masses. Each cycle focuses primarily on one of the synoptic Gospels for a whole year. Some readings from John's Gospel are included, especially during Lent and the Easter season.

A Look at the Gospels

Every day at Mass, we always hear a reading from one of the Gospels. So in this section, we'll describe each of the Gospels as a way to begin to "mine the meaning" so that when we hear the priest announce: "A reading from the Gospel of _____" we'll have some ground into which the seeds of the particular Gospel can be sown. This is a good starting place to begin to mine the meaning.

It is always a good thing to prepare to go to Mass by reading the Gospel and begin to think about it and pray about God's meaning for us.

MARK

Mark's was the first and the shortest of the Gospels to be written. He wrote about the year 70 CE. (CE are the initials for "Common Era"; and these initials mean the same thing as AD or *Anno Domini*, year of our Lord. Using CE is more universal, as it can be used by all people in the world, of all religions). This was around the time when the Romans destroyed the Jewish Temple in Jerusalem. This was a very dangerous time for Christians. In Rome, many Christians were singled out, tortured, and put to death.

This danger made Mark's community full of fear as they questioned their following of Jesus. They must have asked who Jesus really was, and was their commitment really "worth it?"

Mark 's Gospel answers both questions: Jesus is the Messiah (this word means "Savior"), for sure, but a Messiah who would suffer and die for the good of all. For those who are baptized into Christ, there will also be suffering. The Good News is: there is resurrection.

MATTHEW

Matthew's community was composed mostly of Jews who had come to follow Jesus as the "new way." He wrote in the mid-80s of the first century and tried to reassure the people that Jesus had deep ties to the history of the Jewish people and to their traditions.

Matthew's Jesus is a master teacher (the meaning of the title "rabbi"), one who spoke and acted with authority. The meaning of the title "disciple" is a "learner." In Matthew's Gospel, the disciples learn by listening to the words of Jesus and watching him in his actions. After the resurrection in Matthew's Gospel, the disciples are sent out to "make disciples of all nations." In this way, the author of the Gospel reminds the Jewish people that the call to follow Jesus goes out to the whole world.

LUKE Luke's first hearers were a gentile community—which means they were not Jewish. Like Matthew, Luke's Gospel was written in the mid-80s. For this community, Luke highlights some important meanings: the compassion of Jesus, his outreach to the poor, his role as a prophet, and the table as the center of life.

Like a magnet, Jesus draws the poor, the outcast, the sick, women, and foreign people to himself for healing. There are three important parables found only in Luke: the lost sheep, the lost coin, and the lost son (all in chapter 15) that challenge us to reach out to seek and save the lost.

Luke compares Jesus to the prophet Isaiah, as one who heals the sick, releases prisoners, proclaims good news to the poor. Jesus is clearly a prophet as one who is "mighty in deed and in word."

In Luke's Gospel, Jesus dies as he lived: forgiving those who have put him to death, and saving the repentant who is crucified alongside him. Jesus is a healer to the end.

JOHN John's Gospel is different from the other three that share so much in common. John's is the Gospel of the "new creation" and emphasizes the close relationship between Jesus and the Father.

Like the Book of Genesis, John's Gospel begins with the words: "In the beginning..." And John goes on to tell of seven "signs" or miracles, like the days of creation. These signs are done so that we may believe that Jesus is God and one with the Father and the Holy Spirit.

In John's Gospel, the disciples are no longer students but friends. They are a community of Jesus' friends who share the life of Jesus because they share the Holy Spirit. They are to be known because of the love they have for one another. They are to love as Jesus has loved them. Jesus' death is the ultimate sign of his love.

In John's Gospel especially, love is expressed through service. The story of the Last Supper in John is the story of the washing of the feet, where Jesus says: "Do you see what I have done for you? So, you must do for one another." Since John's Gospel was written later and the Eucharist was more developed and commonly practiced, he did not have to retell the story of the bread and wine becoming Jesus' Body and Blood. So John explained the Eucharist in a different way, focusing on it as the bread of life, the body of Christ.

THE NEXT BOOKS

The next book in the Christian Scriptures is the Acts of the Apostles, or "Acts" for short. Acts tells the story of the early Church, how it grew, and even how it struggled following the death and resurrection of Jesus.

After Acts, we have the letters. Most of them were written by Saint Paul. He had brought the Gospel message of Jesus to a number of towns, and he wrote back to them while he was still traveling. He wrote his letters to teach, to challenge, and to encourage the new churches, even though he wasn't physically with them. The "letters" in the Bible are named for the communities who received them.

There are other letters after Saint Paul's, and then we reach the last book of the Bible, Revelation. This is the most difficult book to understand. It uses symbolism from the early Church, a "secret code" of sorts, because it was written in a time of persecution. It was a time when it was not easy or sometimes even safe to be a Christian. Difficult books like Revelation mean we continue to try to "mine" the real meaning.

Bible book names

OLD TESTAMENT

#	Biblical Book	Abbreviation	#	Biblical Book	Abbreviation
1	Genesis	Gn	25	Ecclesiastes or Qoheleth	Eccl
2	Exodus	Ex	26	Song of Songs or Canticle of Canticles	Song
3	Leviticus	Lv	27	Wisdom (of Solomon)	Wis
4	Numbers	Nm	28	Sirach or Ecclesiasticus	Sir
5	Deuteronomy	Dt	29	Isaiah	Is
6	Joshua	Jos	30	Jeremiah	Jer
7	Judges	Jgs	31	Lamentations	Lam
8	Ruth	Ru	32	Baruch	Bar
9	1 Samuel	1 Sm	33	Ezekiel	Ez
10	2 Samuel	2 Sm	34	Daniel	Dn
11	1 Kings	1 Kgs	35	Hosea	Hos
12	2 Kings	2 Kgs	36	Joel	Jl
13	1 Chronicles	1 Chr	37	Amos	Am
14	2 Chronicles	2 Chr	38	Obadiah	Ob
15	Ezra	Ezr	39	Jonah	Jon
16	Nehemiah	Neh	40	Micah	Mi
17	Tobit	Tb	41	Nahum	Na
18	Judith	Jdt	42	Habakkuk	Hb
19	Esther	Est	43	Zephaniah	Zep
20	1 Maccabees	1 Mc	44	Haggai	Hg
21	2 Maccabees	2 Mc	45	Zechariah	Zec
22	Job	Jb	46	Malachi	Mal
23	Psalms	Ps (pl. Pss)			
24	Proverbs	Prv			

NEW TESTAMENT

#	Biblical Book	Abbreviation	#	Biblical Book	Abbreviation
1	Matthew	Mt	14	2 Thessalonians	2 Thes
2	Mark	Mk	15	1 Timothy	1 Tm
3	Luke	Lk	16	2 Timothy	2 Tm
4	John	Jn	17	Titus	Ti
5	Acts of the Apostles	Acts	18	Philemon	Phlm
6	Romans	Rom	19	Hebrews	Heb
7	1 Corinthians	1 Cor	20	James	Jas
8	2 Corinthians	2 Cor	21	1 Peter	1 Pt
9	Galatians	Gal	22	2 Peter	2 Pt
10	Ephesians	Eph	23	1 John	1 Jn
11	Philippians	Phil	24	2 John	2 Jn
12	Colossians	Col	25	3 John	3 Jn
13	1 Thessalonians	1 Thes	26	Jude	Jude
			27	Revelation (to John) or Apocalypse	Rv

Timeline

OLD TESTAMENTO (OT)
BEFORE COMMON ERA (BCE)

YEAR	BIBLICAL EVENT
1900	Abraham and Sarah
1720	Joseph and his brothers' arrival in Egypt
1250	Moses: The exodus from Egypt and the Ten Commandments
1000	King David
922	Division of the kingdom: North, Israel. South, Judah
721	Fall of the northern kingdom into the hands of the Assyrian Empire
587	Fall of the southern kingdom into the hands of the Persian Empire. Babylonian Exile
539	Return of the exiles from Babylonia to Jerusalem
515-445	Rebuilding of Jerusalem and the second Temple
332	Alexander the Great establishes the Greek Empire, defeats the Persians, and conquers Palestine
167	Revolt of Mathias and the Maccabees against kings of Syria
142-63	Period of independence for Judea
63	Fall of Judea into the hands of the Roman Empire (Emperor Pompeii)
37	Herod the Great rules Judea. He is a descendant of the Hasmoneans/Maccabees. He did not come from the line of King David.

Timeline

NEW TESTAMENT (NT)
COMMON ERA (CE)

YEAR APPROXIMATE	BIBLICAL EVENT
6	Birth of Jesus Christ
26	John the Baptist announces the coming of the Messiah
26-29	Jesus begins his public ministry
30	Crucifixion and resurrection of Jesus
36	The first Christians are persecuted by the Jews
36	Conversion of Saint Paul
70	Jewish followers of Jesus expelled from the Temple; Temple destroyed

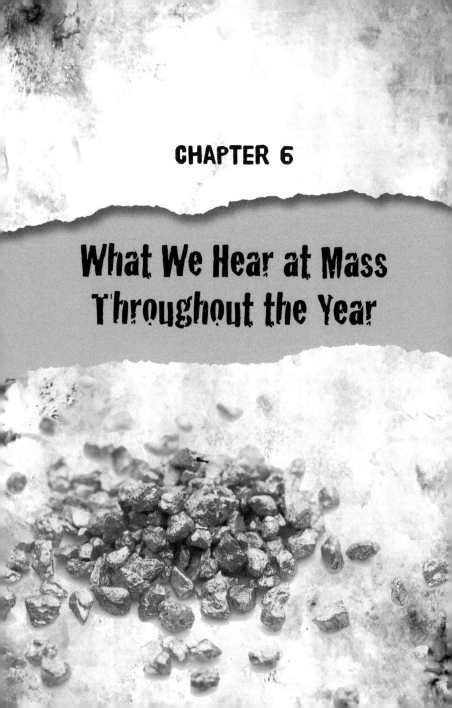

CHAPTER 6

What We Hear at Mass Throughout the Year

Each time we go to Mass, there are always two parts: The Liturgy of the Word and the Liturgy of the Eucharist. Just as with our Jewish ancestors, the *book* is a primary basis of our faith and of our religion. Thus, the Bible, as a library of books, becomes the word of God, our sacred Scripture.

The cycle of the seasons in the Church is known as the liturgical year and focuses primarily on the Sunday Eucharist because Sunday is always remembered as the day of the resurrection of Jesus. We also celebrate Mass every day, but we will focus in this section on the Sunday celebration. Just as families come together for a meal on Sundays, so we, the Christian community, gather for our meal. Just as we share family stories and food at our Sunday dinner, so we Catholic Christians share stories from the Bible and the food of Christ's Body and Blood.

The liturgical year begins every year on the first Sunday of Advent and proceeds through the same cycle of seasons each and every year. So we have:

- Advent and Christmas Time
- Ordinary Time
- Lent and Easter Time
- Pentecost
- Ordinary Time

The colors and decorations in the church and the readings high-light the themes and spirituality of each season.

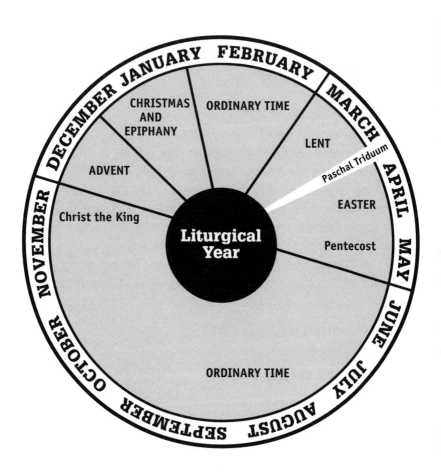

Ordinary Time includes the Sundays when there is no specific event remembered, but the teachings, parables, and miracles of Jesus are recalled for us. And again, it's not enough to simply teach us about Jesus as it is to encourage us to live the Christ life, to do what Jesus would do as we live our lives.

Lent begins on Ash Wednesday and continues through six Sundays before Easter.

After Easter Sunday, we continue to wait for fifty days (the meaning of Pentecost) to remember and celebrate anew the coming of the Holy Spirit.

As mentioned before:

- Cycle A includes readings from Matthew's Gospel
- Cycle B includes readings from Mark's Gospel
- Cycle C includes readings from Luke's Gospel
- Readings from John's Gospel appear mainly in the Lent and Easter seasons.

THE SEASONS OF ADVENT AND CHRISTMAS

In the history of the Church, the season of Advent is celebrated for the four Sundays before Christmas with the singular theme of preparation for the coming of Christ. In the early Church, Advent likely evolved after the season of Lent had been established. Thus, Advent took on a similar penitential theme, as modeled by Lent.

Today we continue to prepare for the coming of Christ. However, we look at three ways that Christ comes: In history as a boy-child born to Mary and Joseph; in the many ways Christ comes to us in our daily lives and prayer; and finally, we await the second coming of Christ in the future. Because Advent leads to the celebration of Christmas, the focus of the season is mainly on the birth of Christ in history.

The first readings at Mass on the Sundays of Advent are drawn from the prophets. In their time, before, during, and after the exile, the prophets speak of the Savior who will be sent by God. It is in hindsight that we know the Savior to be Jesus, the Christ.

So, we hear from Isaiah:

7:14...The virgin shall be with child, and bear a son, and shall name him Emmanuel.

9:1...The people who walked in darkness have seen a great light; upon those who dwell in the land of gloom a light has shone.

9:5...For a child is born to us; a son is given us; upon his shoulder dominion rests. They name him Wonder-Counselor, God-Hero, Father-Forever, Prince of Peace.

11:1–2...A shoot shall sprout from the stump of Jesse, and from his roots a bud shall blossom. The spirit of the Lord shall rest on him, a spirit of wisdom and of understanding, a spirit of counsel and strength, a spirit of knowledge and of fear of the Lord.

11:6...Then the wolf shall be a guest of the lamb, and the leopard shall lie down with the kid. The calf and the young lion shall browse together, with a little child to guide them.

And the second readings also cause us to be patient in our waiting, as with this text from James 5:7–8:

Be patient...until the coming of the Lord. See how the farmer awaits the precious fruit of the earth, being patient with it until it receives the early and the late rains. You too must be patient. Make your hearts firm because the coming of the Lord is at hand.

During Christmas Time, we want to be careful to read/hear the stories of the birth of Christ found in Matthew and in Luke. They are quite different because of the people for whom they were written and the particular messages they impart. If there were background music as we hear Matthew's story, it might be the dramatic music that accompanies the movie *Jaws*. And, for Luke, there is great joy and glory as in the traditional hymn *Joy to the World*.

Matthew's story includes the genealogy of Jesus, the birth of Jesus and the visit of the Magi. Remember that Matthew wrote for the Jewish followers of the "new way" of

> **IF THERE WERE BACKGROUND MUSIC PLAYING AS WE HEAR MATTHEW'S STORY, IT MIGHT BE SOMETHING DRAMATIC.**

Jesus. So Matthew's intent is to assure his hearers that Jesus is the Messiah: a true son of Abraham in the list of ancestors. The birth of Jesus in Matthew's account focuses on Joseph. There is surely a connection with the story of Joseph from Genesis, who also was a dreamer and saw his dreams as a way of hearing from God. And the visit of the Magi awakens the Jewish Christians to the mission of Jesus beyond Jewish boundaries as the wise ones from the East came searching out the Messiah. Upon finding him, they do him homage and offer gifts.

Luke's story includes the annunciation to Mary by Gabriel, Mary's visit to Elizabeth, the birth of Jesus, and the visit of the shepherds. Luke makes it clear that the child to be born is of the Holy Spirit, the Son of God. And, Mary plays an important role in her acceptance of Gabriel's message, "let what you have said be done." Luke's story of the birth of Jesus in a manger is the story we know so well; and the announcement of the birth to the shepherds is met with the joy of "glory to God in heaven, and on earth peace."

The season of Christmas Time concludes with the feast of the Baptism of the Lord. And, we hear the Gospel of the Baptism of Jesus by John in the Jordan. It is an overture and introduction to the public life of Jesus.

ORDINARY TIME

The Sundays of Ordinary Time are numbered. On each Sunday, we continue to hear the stories of the life of Jesus: his ministry and special care for the poor and the sick, his teaching and use of parables, and his miracles. Like the two on the road to Emmaus at the conclusion of Luke's Gospel who said: "Were not our hearts burning within us as he walked with us on the road and explained the Scriptures to us?" Our hearts, too, are set on fire as we mine the meaning of the word we are given to hear.

THE SEASON OF LENT

In written music, composers sometimes add a direction of *lento*, which means, "go slowly." The same is true of the season of Lent, when the whole Church goes slowly to reflect on the meaning of Christ's life and our life in Christ. It is likely that Lent developed from the practice in the early Church of the immediate preparation of catechumens for initiation into the Church at the Easter Vigil. As the already baptized members of the Church accompanied the catechumens, they too reflected on their baptismal commitment. Thus, the season of going slowly emerged as a season of reflection and penitence so that their own commitment to Christ would be renewed at the great Vigil.

IN WRITTEN MUSIC, COMPOSERS SOMETIMES ADD A DIRECTION OF *LENTO*, WHICH MEANS, "GO SLOWLY."

Beginning with Ash Wednesday and continuing for the six Sundays of Lent, the faithful members of the Church hear Gospels that point to the death and resurrection of Jesus that we recall at the great Triduum.

THE EASTER TRIDUUM

The three days recalled at the Triduum are the great mysteries of faith: the Mass of the Lord's Supper (Holy Thursday), the Passion, (Good Friday), and the Mass of the Lord's Resurrection (Holy Saturday). The readings of these all-important days are heard and taken to heart.

At the Mass of the Lord's Supper on Holy Thursday, we hear John's account of the Last Supper, the story of the washing of the feet. We hear and see the servant Jesus, washing the feet of the disciples. He says: do you see what I have done for you? So you must also do. This priest who provides us his own body and blood reminds us that we, too, are called to serve as he has served.

On Good Friday, we gather to hear the story of the passion and death of Jesus from John's Gospel.

At the great Easter Vigil, we celebrate the saving acts of God throughout history and find the climax in the resurrection of Jesus. As a Church, we proclaim that Jesus Christ is risen, and we respond with "Alleluia!"

EASTER SEASON AND PENTECOST

Throughout the fifty days of Easter, we hear the stories that occur after the resurrection of Jesus, the various stories of the disciples' encounters of Jesus alive. In each of the Gospels, the risen Jesus brings peace. Before his ascension to heaven, Jesus promises the advocate who will abide with those who believe. And, in the Acts of the Apostles, we find the story of the coming of the Holy Spirit. This event "fires up" the disciples to spread the word of Jesus, to go forth baptizing in the name of the Father, Son, and Holy Spirit.

At Pentecost, we celebrate the mission of the Church: to spread the Gospel, to build up the body of Christ on earth.

After Pentecost, we return to Ordinary Time. But this time is anything but ordinary as we continue to hear over and over again the stories of Jesus that are the Gospels.

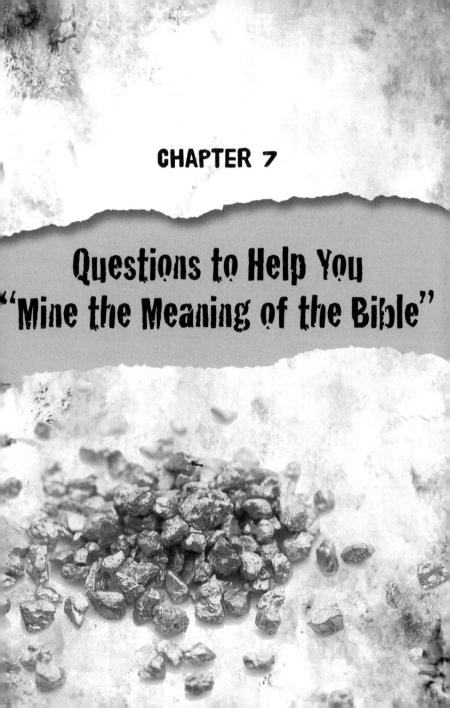

CHAPTER 7

Questions to Help You "Mine the Meaning of the Bible"

Because we live in a world that places great importance on information and knowledge, we are always tempted to ask: "What really happened?" People today are very linear and literal. We equate truth with historical events and vice versa. We often equate story and myth with falsehood and lies. But this is not the world of the Bible, not how the people of the Bible saw and understood their world. When we read or hear the Bible however, we are only seeking "faith data." Even though the Bible is rooted in history, it doesn't always give us factual history. Instead, the Bible gives us stories of faith, stories to stir our souls. The stories set our hearts "burning" within us, just like what happened to the disciples on the road to Emmaus at the end of Luke's Gospel.

So, let us never ask: "What really happened?"

It's always better to ask the next four questions as we seek to "mine the meaning" of the stories in the Bible.

1. What do the words say?

2. What did the story mean to people who heard it first?

3. What does it mean for me and for all of us?

4. What should we do next; what does the Gospel ask of us?

LISTEN CAREFULLY

As you go about the process of answering these questions, first, listen carefully. We are tempted to skip over the beginnings of readings to "get to the good part." However, beginnings are always important, too.

For example, both Matthew and Luke have stories of the birth of Jesus. We call these "infancy" narratives, since they tell about the birth of Jesus. We tend to take the most memorable parts of these two stories, mix them well, and bake them into one story: our Christmas pageant. But there are two stories, and each one has something important to say about the birth of our Lord. There are different meanings highlighted in each of the two stories.

Matthew's Gospel and infancy narrative begin with a genealogy of Jesus—that is, a list of his ancestors. This was very important to the Jews of his time, to know his background and heritage. Matthew then focuses on Joseph, whose story is found in Genesis. This, too, would be important to the Jews who had come to follow Jesus. Matthew also has the story of the Magi, with the important message to the first hearers that Jesus came for all people, like the Magi who came from the East to find Jesus. The Magi story also has the tension with the Roman authorities in the person of Herod. So Matthew's infancy narrative is quite serious and a little tense.

Luke's Gospel is very different. It begins with Elizabeth and Zechariah who, like Abraham and Sarah, were very old and without children. Elizabeth becomes pregnant and gives birth to John the Baptist. It's almost as if Luke says: "If you think God was good in Abraham and Sarah's case, you haven't seen anything yet!" Then in Luke's Gospel, Mary is the primary focus: with Gabriel's annunciation, and the visitation to Elizabeth, the great song of the Magnificat (just like Hannah's song in the book of 1 Samuel) and the birth of Jesus in the manger. Jesus' birth is met with great rejoicing and "glory to God in high heaven, and peace on earth!"

Thus let us be attentive and awake, and intent on mining the meaning.

May we seek to sharpen our listening skills so that we hear the word, starting with all the words we see on the page. Imagine yourself listening to a story. If you're hungry when you hear a story about food, it can feel like that story was meant for you. You might really get into it, or it might just frustrate you and make you hungrier. If you weren't so hungry, maybe you wouldn't listen at all. Who you are—someone who is hungry, full, happy, sad, rich, or poor—makes a difference in how a story sounds to you. Who you are can even change what the story means to you.

THE FIRST "HEARERS"

That's why we have to learn something about the ancient people who heard the Bible's stories when they were first told. We call those people the "first hearers." What were their lives like? What did they hope for? What was hard for them? What worried them? If we get to know who they were, sort of like we get to know a friend after a while, then we'll understand what a story meant to them.

Many people today are searching for and studying their ancestry—that is, their family history. We inherit so much from those who have gone before us. Knowing about them can actually help us to know more about ourselves, about who

> MAY WE SEEK TO SHARPEN OUR LISTENING SKILLS SO THAT WE HEAR THE WORD, STARTING WITH ALL THE WORDS WE SEE ON THE PAGE.

we are. Knowing the stories of the first hearers of the biblical books and stories helps us to know and understand so much more of the meaning that is passed on to us.

Here is an example of how it helps to know about the first hearers. It's from one of the parables that Jesus told. He wanted to give people an idea about the reign of God, so he said: "The reign of God is like a mustard seed..."

That may sound strange to us, but what did it mean to the women and men who heard it way back then? At the time of Jesus, mustard was forbidden in Jewish gardens. So can you imagine the reaction of people when Jesus compared the reign of God to a tiny, forbidden mustard seed? They must have gasped in shock.

Why would Jesus say that? He mentioned it to get the people thinking about what they labeled right and wrong. Were all their laws really in line with God's? By using a mustard seed, his parable became a challenge. We'd never know this without knowing the lives and culture of the "first hearers."

TAKING THE MEANING TO HEART

We all know how we turn to God when things are going wrong. But even when we feel we're at the top of our game, God still challenges us to think and grow. A wise person once said: "The Bible is often used to comfort the troubled; may it also be used to trouble the comfortable." In good times and bad, God is always reaching out to you through the Bible.

In fact, everything we read in the Bible means something, but does everything really have to do with us? Yes. We can figure out what it means for us, or for our whole family, or our community, or even the world. The meaning we are searching for is one that we can take to heart.

That's the goal: what is the meaning that we can take to

heart? It's not just about knowing something in our minds, but the Bible's meaning is meant to become part of us, a meaning that we take to our hearts and hold close in our hearts.

So how do we figure it out? Look at the beginning of John's Gospel. It proclaims Jesus is the light of the world, a light no darkness can extinguish. When we hear this, we can ask ourselves questions like this:

- How is Jesus really light for me?
- How is he the light for us, and for our world?
- When does the whole world see it?
- When do I (or my friends or family) see or feel Jesus, the light?
- How do we recognize him?
- What is the darkness that threatens this light, for me or for us...or for our world?

Finally, when you were little, did you have a favorite storybook that you wanted to hear over and over again? Or in the past few years, was there a song that you loved so much you listened to it for months? And even when you weren't listening to the song, it seemed to keep playing in your mind? It is so amazing that when you read or hear something again and again, over time you notice something new, or understand something in a different way, depending on what is going on in your life at the time. The same is true for the Bible. Every time you read or hear it, you understand more deeply.

Once we know what something in the Bible means to us—what it's saying to us right now—we need to figure out what to do with that message. We need to act.

What does the Bible or a particular story ask of us? This is most important, and we often overlook this question because it's hard. We need to respond with growth...to be the "fruit" that is so often mentioned throughout the Bible.

Let's practice with the "light of the world" passage. We might ask ourselves:

- How am I...how are we...how is our whole world called to live in the light of Christ?
- To reflect the light of Christ?
- To be the light of Christ? The answer for each of us is different every single day.

The Bible helps us respond to God in our minds, hearts, and bodies. We listen and read carefully; we think about what it meant to the first hearers; we let it sink in and touch our hearts; we let it guide our words and actions.

Conclusion

We live in a complicated and busy world and lead complicated and busy lives.

The Bible, although written in different times, places, and cultures, has meaning and enlightenment for us even today. Most importantly, the Bible—which was inspired by God—draws us into deeper relationship with God and shows us how to live as people who are baptized in Christ.

We simply need to read and hear the word of God, and listen with our hearts. Each and every one of us needs to mine the meaning of the Bible so that we find deeper meaning in our lives in Christ.

Handbook for Today's Catholic Teen
ISBN: 978-0-7648-1173-9

This best-selling resource for Catholic teenagers covers traditional topics like Catholic doctrine, practices, and prayers, then tackles serious contemporary issues like violence, media, sex, substance abuse, and matters of conscience. Teens will appreciate the *Handbook's* honest, friendly tone; their parents and teachers will appreciate the conversations it starts. Used alone or with the *Handbook for Today's Catholic Teen Activity Notebook,* it's the perfect guide on the journey to Catholic Christian adulthood.

Handbook for Today's Catholic Teen
Activity Notebook
ISBN: 978-0-7648-1378-8

This activity notebook will provide opportunities for readers to carry out something physically and mentally after reading a section of the *Handbook for Today's Catholic Teen.* The notebook provides teachers and group leaders with instruments for discussion and sharing of experiences, ideas, and questions, especially when structured classroom time is lacking.